MONSTERS!
DRAGONS

BY PETER CASTELLANO

HOT TOPICS

Gareth Stevens
PUBLISHING

Please visit our website, www.garethstevens.com. For a free color catalog of all our high-quality books, call toll free 1-800-542-2595 or fax 1-877-542-2596.

Cataloging-in-Publication Data

Castellano, Peter.
Dragons / by Peter Castellano.
p. cm. — (Monsters!)
Includes index.
ISBN 978-1-4824-4086-7 (pbk.)
ISBN 978-1-4824-4087-4 (6-pack)
ISBN 978-1-4824-4088-1 (library binding)
1. Dragons — Juvenile literature. I. Castellano, Peter. II. Title.
GR830.D7 C38 2016
398'.469—d23

First Edition

Published in 2016 by
Gareth Stevens Publishing
111 East 14th Street, Suite 349
New York, NY 10003

Copyright © 2016 Gareth Stevens Publishing

Designer: Samantha DeMartin
Editor: Kristen Nelson

Photo credits: Background iulias/Shutterstock.com; caption boxes Azuzi/Shutterstock.com; text frames Dmitry Natashin.Shutterstock.com; cover, p. 1 Coneyl Jay/Stone/Getty Images; p. 5 lineartestpilot/Shutterstock.com; p. 7 Trajan 117/Wikimedia Commons; p. 9 Linda Bucklin/Shutterstock.com; p. 11 Print Collector/Hulton Archive/Getty Images; p. 13 windmoon/Shutterstock.com; p. 15 Gitanna/Shutterstock.com; p. 17 Fotokostic/ Shutterstock.com; p. 19 Fine Art Images/Heritage Images/Hulton Archive/Getty Images; p. 21 Sergey Uryadnikov/Shutterstock.com; p. 23 Styve Reineck/Shutterstock.com; p. 24 Ryan Ladbrook/Shutterstock.com; p. 25 kkaplin/Shutterstock.com; p. 27 Torsten Blackwood/AFP/Getty Images; p. 29 ChinaFotoPress/ChinaFotoPress/Getty Images; p. 30 (Lindworm) Interpixels/Shutterstock.com; p. 30 (Lung) Chris 73/Wikimedia Commons; p. 30 (Coca) Catalunyaesunanacio/Wikimedia Commons.

Printed in the United States of America

CPSIA compliance information: Batch #CW16GS: For further information contact Gareth Stevens, New York, New York at 1-800-542-2595.

CONTENTS

MORE THAN A MONSTER

When you imagine a dragon, does it breathe fire? Maybe you picture a friendly dragon, or perhaps it looks like a snake. How you think of a dragon likely depends on your **culture** and the **myths** you've heard about this monster!

BEYOND THE MYTH

It's believed that dragon myths came about independently in Asia and Europe and possibly South America and Australia, too.

DRAGONS IN CHINA

Dragons have been a part of Chinese culture for thousands of years. However, in their myths, dragons aren't monsters! They're very powerful, but they often bring life and good fortune. In fact, the Chinese long believed they were **descendants** of dragons.

BEYOND THE MYTH

Until 1911, the Chinese flag featured a dragon.

Dragons in ancient myths, including those from China, often had a serpentine, or snakelike, body. Chinese dragons lived in lakes, oceans, and rivers. They were believed to live underwater all winter and then bring the rains in the spring.

BEYOND THE MYTH

Ancient people treated illness with "dragon bone" or "dragon's blood." Of course, neither was what it was said to be!

The ancient Chinese so honored the dragon that they began calling the emperor, or ruler, the "true dragon" more than 2,000 years ago. His **throne** was called the "Dragon Throne," and he wore yellow robes with dragons on them.

BEYOND THE MYTH

Chinese emperors gave nearby Asian rulers beautiful dragon robes. This was one way the dragon myth spread to countries such as Vietnam, Borneo, and Japan!

10

11

OTHER ASIAN DRAGONS

Japanese dragons could grow or shrink—or even disappear! In Vietnam, a myth says a dragon that kept the country safe created the islands of Ha Long Bay. According to a story from Borneo, a dragon lives on top of the country's Mount Kinabalu.

BEYOND THE MYTH

Chinese communities around the world make colorful dragons to be used in parades to celebrate their new year, which occurs sometime during January or February, depending on the moon.

TERRIBLE DRAGONS

So where did the idea of dragons as monsters come from? Europe! Myths from the **Middle Ages** include evil, dangerous dragons that look like huge lizards with wings. They breathe fire and sometimes even eat people!

BEYOND THE MYTH

Ancient Roman writer Pliny the Elder wrote about a "dragon" he saw in India. People now believe he may have seen one of the huge pythons that live there. To a visitor, they're pretty monstrous!

15

English legends, or stories, are full of brave knights fighting dragons to save helpless noblewomen and towns. In *Beowulf*, the heroic Beowulf fights a dragon that could kill all his people. Beowulf's big dragon battle had a great effect on later stories.

BEYOND THE MYTH

One legend from about AD 1250 tells of a Swiss knight killing a dragon. However, he then died from touching its blood, which was poisonous.

SYMBOLS OF EVIL

Many faiths have long used snakes and dragons as symbols, or things that stand for something else. In Christian stories, snakes and dragons symbolize evil. The slaying, or killing, of a dragon means removing evil from the world.

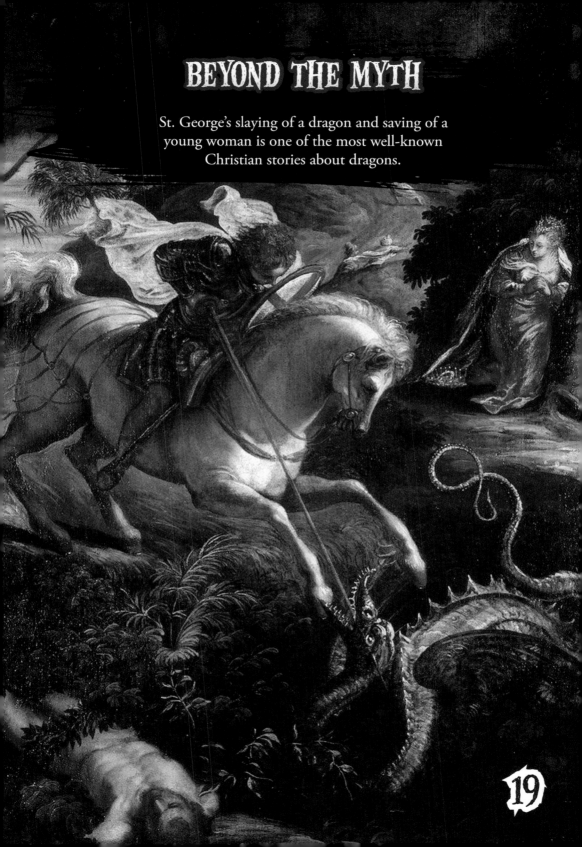

BEYOND THE MYTH

St. George's slaying of a dragon and saving of a young woman is one of the most well-known Christian stories about dragons.

COULD THEY BE REAL?

Even after the Middle Ages, the idea of terrible, huge dragons continued. In fact, people thought they were real! Dragons were thought to be part of the snake and reptile family. Their homes and habits were studied and written about!

BEYOND THE MYTH

Like reptiles, dragons are often pictured as
having scales covering their body. Reptiles are
animals—such as lizards and turtles—that
are cold-blooded and lay eggs.

Imagine hearing stories of dragons all your life and then coming across the huge remains of a dinosaur. Since people centuries ago didn't know about dinosaurs, they believed these big bones were from dragons! This made the stories seem truer.

BEYOND THE MYTH

Scientist Henry Gee concluded that if dragons were real, it wasn't unbelievable that they could breathe fire. A beetle exists that does something like that!

Some real animals likely spread dragon myths. The huge Nile crocodile may have once swum from its home in Africa to Greece or Italy, scaring all those who saw it. Big Australian lizards called goannas also look the part.

BEYOND THE MYTH

Today, animals sometimes have "dragon" in their name! Both the frilled dragon and the bearded dragon are small lizards found in Australia.

BEARDED DRAGON

FRILLED DRAGON

25

POP CULTURE DRAGONS

Today, books and movies do what myths once did —and dragons are still a big part of them! Smaug is a gold-loving dragon guarding a mountain full of treasure in J. R. R. Tolkien's *The Hobbit* and the movies based on it.

BEYOND THE MYTH

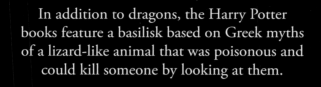

In addition to dragons, the Harry Potter
books feature a basilisk based on Greek myths
of a lizard-like animal that was poisonous and
could kill someone by looking at them.

The movie *How to Train Your Dragon* brings back the idea that many dragons are friendly. Mushu, a dragon in *Mulan*, is also a good dragon in the tradition of Asian dragons. Even today, not all dragons are monsters!

BEYOND THE MYTH

In the *Dragon Ball* series, there are many dragons, including two that grant wishes!

29

Dragon Myths
Around the World

COCA
Portugal
the dragon who fights St. George

LINDWORM
Austria
serpent prince

TIAMAT
Middle East
takes part in creation myth

LUNG
China
symbol of power

BOLLA
Albania
sleeps all year and eats the first person it sees when it wakes up

FOR MORE INFORMATION

BOOKS

Baltzer, Rochelle. *Monsters and Other Mythical Creatures.*
Minneapolis, MN: Magic Wagon, 2015.

Sautter, Aaron. *A Field Guide to Dragons, Trolls, and Other
Dangerous Monsters.* Mankato, MN: Capstone Press, 2015.

WEBSITES

Dragon Facts

kidskonnect.com/animals/dragon/

Find out fun facts about dragons, and explore other links.

Dragons of Ancient Greece

www.theoi.com/greek-mythology/dragons.html

Read about the many dragons and other beasts in ancient
Greek myths.

GLOSSARY

culture: the beliefs and ways of life of a group of people

descendant: a person who comes after another in a family

Middle Ages: a time in European history from about AD 500 to about AD 1500

myth: a legend or story

throne: the seat of a ruler

INDEX